EXPLORE THE UNITED STATES

MICHIGAN

Julie Murray

Big Buddy Books

An Imprint of Abdo Publishing
abdobooks.com

abdobooks.com

Published by Abdo Publishing, a division of ABDO, PO Box 398166, Minneapolis, Minnesota 55439.
Copyright © 2020 by Abdo Consulting Group, Inc. International copyrights reserved in all countries.
No part of this book may be reproduced in any form without written permission from the publisher.
Big Buddy Books™ is a trademark and logo of Abdo Publishing.

Printed in the United States of America, North Mankato, Minnesota
102019
012020

 THIS BOOK CONTAINS
RECYCLED MATERIALS

Design: Aruna Rangarajan, Mighty Media, Inc.
Production: Mighty Media, Inc.
Editor: Liz Salzmann

Cover Photograph: Shutterstock Images
Interior Photographs: AP Images, p. 21; Davel5957/iStockphoto, p. 9 (top left); Denyshutter/
    iStockphoto, p. 30 (middle); Frank Gunn/AP Images, p. 27 (top left); Getty Images, p. 9 (top right);
    Mark LoMoglio/AP Images, pp. 18, 19, 27 (top right); North Wind Picture Archives/Alamy Stock
    Photo, p. 13; Patrick Gorski/Icon Sportswire/AP Images, p. 29 (bottom right); Shutterstock Images,
    pp. 4, 5, 6, 7, 9, 10, 11, 14, 15, 17, 22, 23, 24, 25, 26, 28, 29, 30; smontgom65/iStockphoto, p. 10
    (inset); Wikimedia Commons, pp. 20, 26 (bottom right), 27

Populations figures from census.gov

Library of Congress Control Number: 2019943207

Publisher's Cataloging-in-Publication Data

Names: Murray, Julie, author.
Title: Michigan / by Julie Murray
Description: Minneapolis, Minnesota : Abdo Publishing, 2020 | Series: Explore the United States |
    Includes online resources and index.
Identifiers: ISBN 9781532191251 (lib. bdg.) | ISBN 9781532177989 (ebook)
Subjects: LCSH: U.S. states--Juvenile literature. | Midwest States--Juvenile literature. | Physical
    geography--United States--Juvenile literature. | Michigan--History--Juvenile literature.
Classification: DDC 977.4--dc23

CONTENTS

ONE NATION

The United States is a diverse country. It has farmland, cities, coasts, and mountains. Its people come from many different backgrounds. And, its history covers more than 200 years.

Today the country includes 50 states. Michigan is one of these states. Let's learn more about Michigan and its story!

DID YOU KNOW?

Michigan became a state on January 26, 1837. It was the twenty-sixth state to join the nation.

Most of Michigan is surrounded by four of the five Great Lakes. These are Lakes Superior, Michigan, Huron, and Erie.

CHAPTER 2

MICHIGAN UP CLOSE

The United States has four main regions. Michigan is in the Midwest.

Michigan has three states on its borders. Wisconsin is west. Indiana and Ohio are south. The country of Canada borders Michigan to the east. But, most of Michigan is bordered by water!

Michigan has a total area of 96,713 square miles (250,486 sq km). About 9.9 million people live there.

Puerto Rico became a US commonwealth in 1952.

DID YOU KNOW?

Washington, DC, is the US capital city. Puerto Rico is a US commonwealth. This means it is governed by its own people.

★ Regions of ★
the United States

West
Midwest
South
Northeast

CANADA

WASHINGTON
OREGON
MONTANA
IDAHO
WYOMING
CALIFORNIA
NEVADA
UTAH
COLORADO
ARIZONA
NEW MEXICO

NORTH DAKOTA
SOUTH DAKOTA
NEBRASKA
KANSAS
OKLAHOMA
TEXAS

MINNESOTA
WISCONSIN
IOWA
MISSOURI
ILLINOIS
INDIANA
MICHIGAN
OHIO
KENTUCKY
TENNESSEE
ARKANSAS
ALABAMA
GEORGIA
MISSISSIPPI
LOUISIANA
FLORIDA

NEW HAMPSHIRE
VERMONT
MAINE
PENNSYLVANIA
NEW YORK
MASSACHUSETTS
RHODE ISLAND
CONNECTICUT
NEW JERSEY
DELAWARE
MARYLAND
WASHINGTON, DC
WEST VIRGINIA
VIRGINIA
NORTH CAROLINA
SOUTH CAROLINA

PACIFIC OCEAN

MEXICO

ALASKA
HAWAII
PUERTO RICO

Gulf of Mexico

ATLANTIC OCEAN

N
W E
S

7

CHAPTER 3

IMPORTANT CITIES

Lansing is Michigan's capital. It is an industrial city. Michigan State University is located nearby in East Lansing.

Detroit is the state's largest city. It is home to 672,662 people. It is known as "Motor City" because many cars are made there.

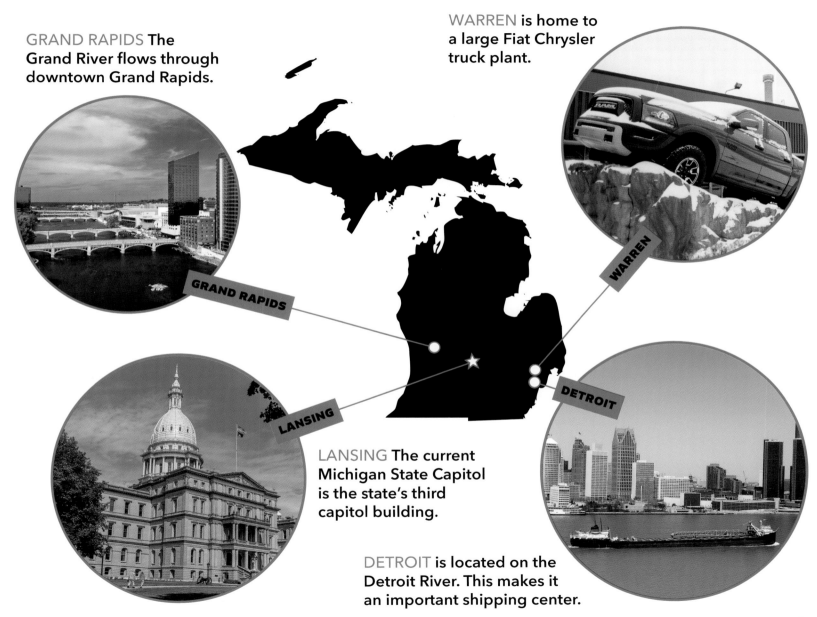

GRAND RAPIDS The Grand River flows through downtown Grand Rapids.

WARREN is home to a large Fiat Chrysler truck plant.

GRAND RAPIDS

WARREN

LANSING

DETROIT

LANSING The current Michigan State Capitol is the state's third capitol building.

DETROIT is located on the Detroit River. This makes it an important shipping center.

Grand Rapids is Michigan's second-largest city. It is home to 200,217 people. Many products are made in this industrial city.

Warren is the state's third-largest city. It has 134,587 people. This city is part of the Detroit metropolitan area. Many cars and car parts are made there.

DID YOU KNOW?

US president Gerald Ford grew up in Grand Rapids. The Gerald R. Ford Presidential Museum is located there. Ford and his wife, Betty, are buried on the museum grounds.

The Ambassador Bridge connects Detroit and Windsor, Ontario, Canada. It is a busy trade route between the United States and Canada.

CHAPTER 4

MICHIGAN IN HISTORY

Michigan's history includes Native Americans and settlers. Native Americans have lived in present-day Michigan for thousands of years. In about 1620, a French explorer visited the area. Over time, the French claimed and settled the land. In 1701, Detroit was founded. People traded goods there.

By 1783, the United States controlled the Michigan area. A waterway called the Erie Canal was finished in 1825. Then, boats could easily reach Michigan from the east. So, more people began moving there. In 1837, Michigan became a state.

French trader Antoine Laumet de La Mothe Cadillac founded Detroit.

CHAPTER 5

ACROSS THE LAND

Michigan is divided into two parts by Lake Michigan. The land north of the lake is called the Upper Peninsula. In the west, it has rocky hills, mountains, and cliffs. In the east, it has low swamps. The land east of the lake is called the Lower Peninsula. It has sand dunes, rolling hills, and farmland.

Many types of animals make their homes in Michigan. These include deer, bears, ducks, turkeys, and moose. Whitefish and trout are found in the Great Lakes.

DID YOU KNOW?
In July, the average high temperature in Michigan is 80°F (26.6°C). In January, it is 29°F (-1.6°C).

Many parts of Michigan have forests. The state also has about 11,000 lakes.

CHAPTER 6

EARNING A LIVING

Michigan is known for farming and industry. Farms produce fruits, vegetables, and dairy. Many factories make automobiles and metal products.

Michigan is a popular vacation spot. So, many people have jobs helping visitors. Other people work in mines. The state provides limestone, gravel, and sand.

About three-fourths of the country's tart cherries are grown in Michigan.

CHAPTER 7

SPORTS PAGE

Many people think of sports when they think of Michigan. Detroit teams play baseball, hockey, basketball, and football.

College sports are also popular in the state. The University of Michigan is known for football. And, Michigan State University is known for basketball.

The University of Michigan football team won the Citrus Bowl in 2016! The team beat the University of Florida 41 to 7.

CHAPTER 8

HOMETOWN HEROES

Many famous people are from Michigan. Henry Ford was born in Wayne County in 1863. In 1903, he started the Ford Motor Company. In 1908, he created the Model T car. Ford found a way to build the Model T faster and cheaper than other cars.

Charles Lindbergh was born in Detroit in 1902. He was famous for flying airplanes. In 1927, he made the first nonstop one-person airplane flight across the Atlantic Ocean!

DID YOU KNOW?
The Model T was one of the first cars that many people could afford. It helped change the way Americans traveled!

Lindbergh flew from New York City to Paris, France, in 33.5 hours. His plane was called the *Spirit of St. Louis.*

Diana Ross was born in Detroit in 1944. In the 1960s, she was the lead singer for the group The Supremes. In 1970, Ross left the group and released many hit songs as a solo artist. She also starred in several movies.

Serena Williams was born in Saginaw in 1981. She became one of the best tennis players in the world. Williams has won 23 major tournaments in singles. She also has four Olympic gold medals!

Williams is known for playing a very powerful style of tennis.

CHAPTER 9

A GREAT STATE

The story of Michigan is important to the United States. The people and places that make up this state offer something special to the country. Together with all the states, Michigan helps make the United States great.

Mackinac Bridge connects Michigan's Upper and Lower Peninsulas. It is 8,344 feet (2,543 m) long.

Sleeping Bear Dunes National Lakeshore is a popular vacation area. More than 1 million people visit each year.

TIMELINE

1837

Michigan became the twenty-sixth state on January 26.

1887

The now-famous Grand Hotel opened on Mackinac Island.

1903

Henry Ford founded the Ford Motor Company in Detroit.

1800s

Lansing became the state **capital**.

1847

Ransom Olds started the Olds Motor Vehicle Company in Lansing. It made popular cars called Oldsmobiles.

1897

The first Tulip Time Festival was held in Holland, Michigan. The city grew 100,000 tulips!

1929

1959

Berry Gordy Jr. started Motown Records in Detroit. Motown grew famous for hit music by African American singers. These included Diana Ross and Stevie Wonder.

2008

The Detroit Red Wings hockey team won their eleventh Stanley Cup!

2016

The University of Michigan football team won the Citrus Bowl.

1900s

2000s

Gerald Ford of Grand Rapids became the thirty-eighth US president.

1974

More than 800,000 gallons (3 million L) of oil spilled in the Kalamazoo River near Marshall. It was one of the Midwest's worst oil spills.

2010

27

TOUR BOOK

Do you want to go to Michigan? If you visit the state, here are some places to go and things to do!

SEE
Visit the city of Holland in May for the Tulip Time Festival. It is one of the largest US flower festivals!

VISIT
Spend time on Mackinac Island. No cars are allowed there. Instead, you can walk, bike, or ride in horse-drawn carriages.

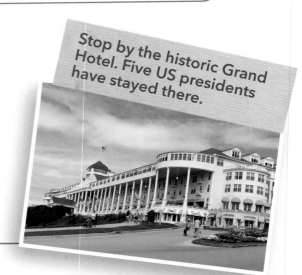

Stop by the historic Grand Hotel. Five US presidents have stayed there.

EXPLORE

Tour Pictured Rocks National Lakeshore on Lake Superior. It is known for multicolored rock. Sandstone cliffs rise up to 200 feet (61 m) above the water.

Visit the Au Sable Light Station. It has been in use since 1874.

CHEER

Catch a University of Michigan versus Michigan State University game. It is exciting to see these rivals play football, basketball, and other sports!

DISCOVER

Visit the Henry Ford Museum of American Innovation in Dearborn. The museum includes amazing historic exhibits. You can also ride in a real Model T car, tour a car factory, and more.

29

FAST FACTS

▶ STATE FLOWER
Apple Blossom

▶ STATE TREE
White Pine

▶ STATE BIRD
American Robin

▶ STATE FLAG:

▶ NICKNAMES:
Wolverine State, Great Lake State

▶ DATE OF STATEHOOD:
January 26, 1837

▶ POPULATION (RANK):
9,995,915
(10th most-populated state)

▶ TOTAL AREA (RANK):
96,713 square miles
(11th largest state)

▶ STATE CAPITAL: Lansing

▶ POSTAL ABBREVIATION: MI

▶ MOTTO:
"Si Quaeris Peninsulam Amoenam
Circumspice" (If You Seek a Pleasant
Peninsula, Look About You)

GLOSSARY

capital—a city where government leaders meet.

diverse—made up of things that are different from each other.

dune—a hill or ridge of loose sand piled up by the wind.

industry—the process of using machines and factories to make products.

limestone—a type of white rock used for building.

metropolitan—of or relating to a large city, usually with nearby smaller cities called suburbs.

peninsula—land that sticks out into water and is connected to a larger piece of land.

region—a large part of a country that is different from other parts.

swamp—land that is wet and often covered with water.

ONLINE RESOURCES

Booklinks
NONFICTION NETWORK
FREE! ONLINE NONFICTION RESOURCES

To learn more about Michigan, please visit **abdobooklinks.com** or scan this QR code. These links are routinely monitored and updated to provide the most current information available.

INDEX